The Ant and the Grasshopper

Aesop

Retold by Liana Robinson
Illustrated by Daniela Dogliani

Series Editor Rob Waring

✳ Introduction ✳

This story is by the Greek writer Aesop.

This story teaches us about hard work.

✳ Characters ✳

Ant

Grasshopper

✴ Words to Know ✴

change

corn

grass

save

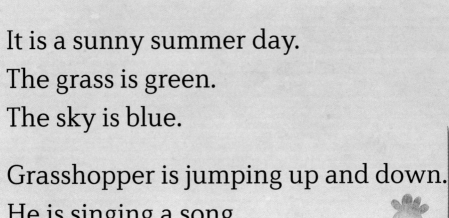

It is a sunny summer day.
The grass is green.
The sky is blue.

Grasshopper is jumping up and down.
He is singing a song.
He is happy.

Grasshopper sees Ant.
She is working hard.
She is finding corn.

"Come talk with me, Ant.
Let's sing a song!" says Grasshopper.

"Work, work, work!
Save, save, save!
There is no time.
Winter is coming!" says Ant.

"Winter? No!
It is a sunny summer day!" says
Grasshopper.

"Come work with me, Grasshopper.
You need food," says Ant.

"Work, work, work!" she says.
"Save, save, save!
 Winter is coming!"

Grasshopper does not work with Ant.
He does not save food for winter.

Ant works hard.
She saves lots of food.

The grass changes.
The trees change.

"Winter is coming!" says Ant.

Winter is cold!

Grasshopper has no food.
He is hungry.

Now Grasshopper knows.
Work, work, work!

Save, save, save!
And you will not be hungry!

✳ Playlet ✳

The Ant and the Grasshopper
Aesop

Cast   Ant, Grasshopper

Scene   **A sunny summer day**

Grasshopper enters singing.

Grasshopper: La-la-la! La-la!

Ant enters.

Ant: Work, work, work! Save, save, save! Winter is coming!

Grasshopper: Winter? No! It's a sunny summer day!

Ant: Come work with me, Grasshopper. You need food for winter.

Grasshopper: No. I want to sing. I want to jump.

Grasshopper exits singing. Ant exits as she looks for food.

Scene **A cold winter day**

Grasshopper enters.

Grasshopper: Brrr! I'm cold! I'm hungry, too. Where is the grass? Where is the food?

Grasshopper exits. Ant enters. She is cooking.

Ant: La-la-la! La-la! I love to sing! La-la-la! La-la! I love to cook!

Somebody is at the door of Ant's house. Ant opens the door.

Ant: Hello, Grasshopper!
Grasshopper: Hello, Ant!

Ant:	Come in! How are you?
Grasshopper:	I'm cold and hungry.
Ant:	It's nice in here. I have lots of food.
Grasshopper:	Yes, now I know. Work, work, work! Save, save, save! And you will not be hungry!
Ant:	Yes. Here. Have some corn.
Grasshopper:	Thank you!
Ant:	Let's sing a song!
Ant and Grasshopper:	La-la-la! La-la! Work, work, work! Save, save, save! And you will not be hungry! La-la-la! La-la!

The End

☀ Story Review ☀

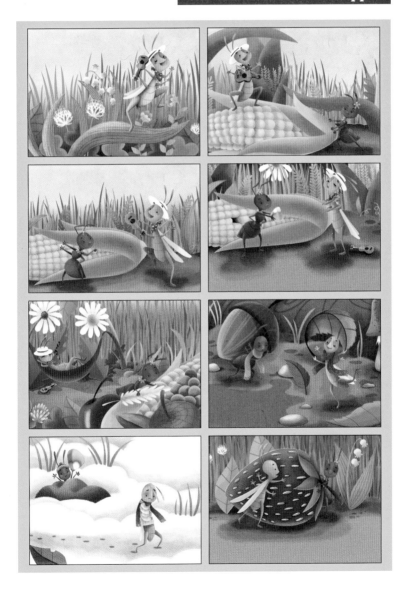

e-future Classic Readers Level S

Levels	Starter	1	2	3	4	5	6
CEFR	A1	A1	A1	A1	A1/A2	A2	A2
Headwords	200	250	350	550	800	1000	1300

S-①	The Princess and the Pea	*Hans Christian Andersen*
S-②	The Ant and the Grasshopper	*Aesop*
S-③	The Fox and the Grapes	*Aesop*
S-④	The Girl in Red	*The Grimm Brothers*
S-⑤	The Girl and the Pot of Milk	*Aesop*
S-⑥	The Fox and the Cat	*Aesop*
S-⑦	The Spring of Youth	*Lafcadio Hearn*
S-⑧	The Lion in Love	*Aesop*
S-⑨	The Two Pots	*Aesop*
S-⑩	The Red Shoes	*Hans Christian Andersen*

S-⑪	Peter and the Wolf	*Sergei Prokofiev*
S-⑫	Snow White	*The Grimm Brothers*
S-⑬	The Ugly Duckling	*Hans Christian Andersen*
S-⑭	The Fox and the Crow	*Aesop*
S-⑮	King of the Cats	*Joseph Jacobs*
S-⑯	Jack	*Joseph Jacobs*
S-⑰	Cupid, the Bad Boy	*Hans Christian Andersen*
S-⑱	How the Rabbit Loses Her Tail	*A South American Folk Tale*
S-⑲	The King with the Golden Touch	*A Greek Myth*
S-⑳	The Rabbit and His Ears	*Aesop*